Also by Susan Herron Sibbet

Poetry

The Weight Is Comforting

Under Suspicion of Sisters

Suspensions (coauthor)

No Easy Light

Poetry and Prose

Burnt Toast and Other Recipes

Fiction

The Constant Listener

Great Blue

Great Blue

Susan Herron Sibbet

Sixteen Rivers Press

Some of the poems in this book previously appeared in *The Weight Is Comforting*, *Under Suspicion of Sisters*, *Burnt Toast and Other Recipes*, and *Suspensions*, all from White Mountain Press, and in *What the World Hears* (California Poets in the Schools Statewide Anthology, 2009) and *VIVO*. "Losing the Way" appeared in *No Easy Light* (Sixteen Rivers Press, 2004) in a different version as "In That Dark Wood."

Special thanks to David Sibbet
and Dina and Daniel DuBois
for their support of this publication.

Published by Sixteen Rivers Press
P.O. Box 640663
San Francisco, CA 94164
www.sixteenrivers.org

Library of Congress Control Number: 2016944124
ISBN: 978-1-939639-11-0

Cover art: *Carmel Cove No. 1*, Carolyn Miller, acrylic on canvas

For Susan's children: Thom, Valentine, Jerda, and Phillip

Contents

Water Is My Only Home

Foreword

My mom was a talker. Everyone knew that about her. She could talk about the small things: the color of an apricot from the CSA farm where she got her fruit every week; the beautiful ruffle of a lettuce leaf; new shoots on a bush in her backyard garden. She could talk about the medium things: what dress to wear for a special occasion, family stories, traveling, and birds, of course. Sometimes she railed against the bureaucrats tangling things up for education and children, reducing funding for the arts again. Sometimes it was Congress, or the writers at the *New York Times*, but there was always something to talk about. She talked about the big things too, though not so much: losing and finding, illness—but these were harder for her and for me, too.

Since she left us, the thing I notice most is the silence. Gone are the phone conversations at odd hours because of our three-hour time difference. Gone are the talks about children and husbands as we sat side by side in lumpy massage chairs getting our matching toes pedicured. "Remember when we realized we had the same feet?" she would ask every time.

I will never forget. The silence is so deep. But then there is her poetry. What strikes me now, reading her most private work—the poems she hardly let anyone but her poetry group see, the ones in the bottom of the desk drawer that have become this book—is how someone with so many words could say so much in so few.

The economy of words in her poetry is the opposite of the words in her daily life. On the page, her words are so carefully chosen, and from each so much is demanded. So many layers and levels of meaning are represented and explored by each. An entire painting can be evoked by one phrase. Such was the beauty of her art, the skill of her construction.

The torrent of her words is gone now, leaving only her wonderful poems to ponder in the silence.

—*Valentine Brown*

Heartland

I Come from the Corner of Walnut and Elm

I know where trees come from:
round green acorns,
light-brown cups that turned dark
in November and the long winter wet.

I know where green wings float
and twirl the maple downhill.
In the bright light
I climbed out on the low porch roof—broad, slanted—
put my head into the leafing branches,
May and summer almost there.

I know where the seedlings sprout
in the scratchy, dry dandelion lawn,
the oak, maples,
teriyaki smoke and highball clink on the porch
and thorns of black locust,
bare summer feet, rough sticky pitch,
the long trunk of the pine
up to a branch I could reach.

I know coal-dust hands,
winter-radiator *clang*, puddles by the door,
bright shadows under the bare trees
too cold and hard
for climbing.

Caesura

The middle daughter   was always anxious
she was missing something   like those breaks
in the middle of old poems   *Beowulf*
she was puzzled   when she first read it
the pause or space   the line balanced
who put it there   was it for breath
a natural break   to speak the long and consonanted line

Some looked at the common   crunched thinginess
all tumbled together   into the tub of sound
and never noticed   the silent center
or how the family   made decisions
balanced in that weighing   the older ones needed
the younger ones had to have   but where was she

Things My Sisters and I Could Do in Summer

We could walk barefoot to the Flying Horse sign.
We could buy a popsicle for a nickel.
We could lie down under the big maple tree.

We could talk about the baby.
We could pretend she was a doll.
We could pretend that we were horses.

We could argue.
We could try to climb the peach trees.
We could hide under the lilac bush and wait for bluebirds.

We could make fairy gardens in the mud under the daylilies.
We could swing out over the road on the long rope swing
and wait for the sound of the car coming back up the hill.

We could cool off lying in the dark
outside on the sleeping porch.
We could try not to sleep.

Edges Like Toast

My grandmother came to us just once
on the train from Oklahoma
with her small black shoes,
her slippery dark dresses.
I wanted to touch her, pat
her smooth round cheeks.
My Herron grandmother stood still
and listened; her silence was
complicated, like the curve
of a small brown egg.
My father's mother, she stood
in the middle of my mother's kitchen
and stirred down the fermenting batter
for her special bread made from potatoes
and cornmeal, my father's favorite.
That small, heavy loaf
of salt-rising bread,
sour and golden yellow,
tasted better toasted, spread
with apple butter.
My grandmother kept
her edges like toast—
rounded, hard, sour—
good as toast,
my Herron grandmother.

Southern Station

For my dad

Freedom was not a song my father sang;
duty was the string to his guitar.
But some warm evenings he would drive us down
to the Southern Station. We'd park and run
to watch the night trains going south.

He held us up to wave and still be safe
beside the huge dark metal valves and wheels.
His arms held us back from the rushing air and roar;
the engine pulled away and left the station lights.

We stayed to watch until the last car passed—
that moving house with its snug curtains, lighted windows.
The caboose! we called. *The caboose!*
and its red light winked down the night.

We drove back on empty streets, past houses
dark except for one flickering silver square.
At home, the baby was asleep,
so we held our voices quiet on the stairs
while our minds raced away.

In 1949

We moved back to Pearl Harbor.
We looked down the hill
past red dirt, green rustling cane fields,
over the water and the gray ships
moving slowly back and forth.

We watched, surrounded by fathers
in their khakis and younger ones in whites.
One war just over, another just beginning,
we didn't mourn, we didn't even speak of the dead.

The Navy offices, the hospital, the dispensary,
were at the end of our street,
and we'd visit our father in his airless office
with its shining linoleum floor
and slowly revolving black metal fan.
CINCPAC Fleet—I loved the name—*Sink Pack Fleet.*
Wouldn't my father's side always win?
And he'd never die?

Years later, I learned what it meant:
Commander in Chief Pacific Fleet.
And we visited the graveyard of more than a thousand men
just there beneath the surface.
No wonder my father never let us swim
in the blue waters of that bay.

Growing Up as a Navy Junior

When the DDT truck came around
every two weeks in summer
in Pearl Harbor,
right before suppertime
at that crazy-still time of day
when the kids had gathered
and run out of things to do,
we'd chase after it,
all of us, in our bare feet,
letting the droplets
of sweet perfumed liquid
scatter before us,
darkening the ground
just ahead
like a sudden warm rain shower
emptying the air.

Heartland

She has come away from the heartland, the ancestral home, leaving the red rounded hills and regular pulse, the ordered seasons. Reluctantly, she drives the long road out, remembering every hurt, blow, word, betrayal, insult, and yet she doesn't want to leave. Driven by the slow ache, weighed down—unreachable, she wants to be unreachable, until the warning light comes on. She stops by the side of the road, hoping the light will go off on its own, as it always has before. She tries her usual fix, but not this time. And so she waits, feeling sick, too full with it, sick of the smell, what was it this time, that too sweet smell of blood, sticky and warm, too much heart. Soon the light will go out, and she will go on, remembering, forgetting, almost.

Losing the Way

In the night wood, I walked blindly
through the empty air, listening for faint voices
drifting up without direction from the path where I wanted to be.

If I had missed the turn, I could have walked for miles, lost;
the forest went on and on. I could not see, and so I slowed
to stare into the complete dark   and staring, it was only darker.

I stopped, afraid to go on, afraid to go back,
and suddenly
                    a shadow from the air just brushed past—
                                                  feathered
                                             flapped

and there in the dark my fear drew back, and I could see.
It was a lifting of the dark, a coming of the light,
coming to me in that dark wood.

Before I Begin

Predator, Thrumming

Warty toads seem almost boneless and are hard to keep in this coastal city. One dark suburban night I brought one home in a box. I wanted him—toads eat snails. I put him down in the garden and he remained, single, without ally or safety in a backyard fenced with well-worn cat walks, fur tufting every knothole. No pools, either; water only darkens the sand before disappearing. I never saw his speckled skin the exact color of strawberry leaves again. And yet I heard him for two springs. We knew it was spring; often in the long dusk I heard his strangely resonant thrumming. Every time that twang loosened its vibrant chord, it stopped me. I imagined him—alien, earless, moist skin—listening, sounding the dark.

The snails still glide everywhere, smoother than sand. I only wish once I could have seen how the soft predacious act was done, how without tooth or claw did he break the shell and feast along the lily leaf.

Bread Haiku

Soft voice of bread—
all afternoon waiting for it to rise,
everything slows.

Toast

I toast warm buttered toast,
toast white bread, wheat-berry,
whole-wheat, dark rye, sourdough toast.
I make toast, and it pops up—
toast!
and sometimes black toast, burnt toast—
a faint plume of toast smoke floats
out into the bedroom. "Toast?"

The crunch and grind of toast teeth,
the toast crust harder than toast itself.
Under eggs, under cream, toast softens.
Lost toast behind the machine
turns gray, turns spotted-toast green:

I toast the whole universe
                                        of toast.

Jam Jars

blackberries stain
blueberries float
apricots turn brown
apple butter spreads out
cream
smooth
cinnamon
dark
changeling

Old China

Old china is never marked
China, like

the broken blue and white bowl,
big pieces loud on the tile floor.

Carefully, I put them in the trash,
wrapping the sharp edges,

wondering,
How can I replace it?

Tiny chips still appearing
the next day.

Please Porridge: Shopping Hints

Shopping cart I got
Shopping cart I rolled
Shopping cart I filled right up
Still no food

One potato tots
Two potatoes cold
Three potatoes dried & bagged
Chopped & fried & rolled

Whitish cabbage bought
Whitish cabbage sold
Cabbage slaw in a package mix
Shredded, dreaded, old

Lettuce in a bag
Lettuce in a ball
White & brown & watery
Lettuce in a bowl

Chips & dips & pop
Cookies, cakes & booze
Cleansers, soap & packaged charm
Toilet paper rolls

Push the basket up
Push the basket down
Fill it up & take it out
Still no food

To the Colma Dump

You have run long enough, run
from their incurable desire,
and still they hunger for you, your
massive cryptic shape,
your smooth blank face.
They have followed you
far from the bright refrigerator showroom
through years of cold white nights
behind the door.
Finally the time has come
for you to lose your door,
to go down past the Driftwood Motel,
down the highway to the Colma dump.

There in the daylight, lie down
among the growing mounds,
three-legged chairs, chipped memorial plates,
bent Venetian blinds.
Lying open, you will remain
hidden but useful, exuding
iron oxide, disintegrating hydrocarbons,
exchanging ions. Fill yourself
with your own contents, no
one's leftovers—
be your own appliance,
become one with the foliate ground.

Ten Poems I Want to Write

1. Unease at the Time Change
2. The Telephone: Enemy or Friend?
3. Family Business
4. Something about Sourdough
5. When I Come into the Empty House
6. Never Begin with the Title (and other stupid things I've said to my students)
7. Falling Asleep on the Sofa
8. The Poem Begins/In Some Uneasy Feeling
9. Why Is the Dark Darker in the Early-Morning Hours?
10. Coffee and Poets

Before I Begin

I am waiting for the change to happen
before I begin.
I am waiting until I have more time.
I am waiting until I have no distractions so I can concentrate.
I am waiting until I learn more about the suffragettes before
I write the 1920s.
I am waiting until I read all the novels written in the '30s before
I write the '30s,
and waiting to read all the war memoirs before I write the '40s.
I am waiting to finish reading all the unexpurgated memoirs
and diaries,
all the sexologists' handbooks,
and all the homoerotic revelations before I write the '50s.
I am waiting to read Anaïs Nin.
I am waiting to read all of Virginia Woolf's novels, diaries,
letters, and journals
and all her family's, all her friends', and everybody else's
memoirs of her.
I am waiting to write *my* memoirs.
I am waiting for the water to boil,
waiting for the coffee to brew.
I am waiting for grounds to settle,
for the coffee to cool.
I am waiting to finish the second cup
before I begin.

I am waiting for the mail to come.
I am waiting for the phone to ring,
waiting for the phone to stop ringing,
for the machine to pick up.
I am waiting for someone to call back.
I am waiting for the beep.
I am waiting for the dog to get in the car before we start.
I am waiting for the traffic to slow and the cars to get by
before I pull out.
I am waiting for them to make a better battery for electric cars.
I am waiting to get revenge on the men who built
the elevated freeways through all the downtowns that were
still alive, and killed them.
I am waiting and listening to my engine idle too fast.
I am waiting to get my car tuned until the day when
I don't have to drive anywhere.
I am waiting for the toll.
I am waiting for the road to clear.
I am waiting for the idea to hit.
I am waiting for the change to happen
before I begin.

Something, Inertia

Sleeping
beside the empty bowl,
the dog waits, and I
stand at the sink
under something—inertia,
            endless dirty dishes—
                dreaming of sand, sky, blue starflowers.

The dishes layer themselves,
alternate blobs of egg, sticky
slick oil dressing.
The forks have something stuck
                between the second and third prong.

The neighbor comes to the door to report
on the cockroaches, the fire
        supposedly set by some children,
                accidentally ours, and
                    the flooded garden, and the landlady.

Our money has flown wings
and flies somewhere over our heads.
I believe in writing checks,
        some form the world waits for.
                        It's in the mail.

Evidence That Couldn't Be Given in Kitsap County, Washington

Bremerton Concrete vs. the Sibbet & Munson Families

The land is its own evidence;
it belongs to itself.
We can clear-cut the lot, try to hold it
in our hands for a while,
but new growth pushes up,
covering the brush piles.

Thick white smoke from alder wood,
wet wood, slash pile, dirt ground
into shreds of cedar bark.
Quick growth of salmonberry
lies across the scar.
Close weave of bramble, black caps,
kinnikinnick rooting in the cedar stump,
the mound softened, small bright leaves upright.

Cedar from the first cut, fifty years ago,
the old growth and the axe mark,
the bark crumbling,
gently running off red,
red cedar melting,
and the dirt turns yellow
where the hornets have built a nest,
and sandy from the tunnels of
the white-footed mouse,

and bear prints big as my hand
press into the black dirt up the road
to the Pope & Talbott clear-cut.

When we try to walk
the boundary corner to corner,
the line bends from the struggle
through slash and growth, looking for
the surveyor's mark:
red and blue plastic ribbons tied
to a young cedar, nailed to a
crooked stump, blown down in the mud.

On paper, the court settled the case;
on paper, the land is ours, as long as
we keep paying,
and the alders are springing
up through the slash,
green and silver across the clearing,
golden in the afternoon light.

When other people were wrong she got such a thrill from it, it frightened her. A rush. She loved to go over every aspect of their wrongness, the misunderstandings that began it—the late message, the missed connection, blaming the kids.

Usually, *she* was wrong. But now, watching X bristle under the wrong, swell with it, it was hard not to feel a quiet fear that maybe this time she was *too* wrong, that or not wrong enough, so they would never work it out, never get to the balanced apologies and explanations, the feelings opened up and shared. Every other time, no matter how it began, she was the one to try to right the wrong, to start to bring it back to the balance point again. But this time in the middle of what had happened, in the confusion of fault finding and blame taking, she didn't know who would return to talking.

Ultimately, who did what ceased to matter except to tell a good story. She was very good at that, and sometimes she wondered how often she was wrong just to get a good story out of it, her own aesthetic demanding that the drama include being wrong.

Hymn: A Sonnet

"I will plant the bulbs today,"
again she lied. They need to be in dirt. For weeks
she'd wanted to, had already taken them out of the cold,
their bags still tied with knotted strings.
The label said, "To you, from Flower Lane.
Plant in early fall." She feared
to see what might remain, just dry
husks and moldy dust inside. Gently
she shook the bag to hear the rustle
of dried blubs. Almost throwing them out
without looking, in some place
where no one would know that she had failed.
Another spring too full and bags of stuff still to do.
Again she sighed, "Today."

Linen Closet

Order is not merely geometrical; it can also remember the family history.
—Gaston Bachelard, from "Drawers, Chests and Wardrobes" in *The Poetics of Space*

Our linen closet is layered, orderly, crowded, with its five shelves, five levels of accessibility, decided not by any logical definition, but simply by the ability of the usual person desiring to remove an item from one of the shelves: that is, by how tall I am.

The lower middle shelf and the bottom need stooping, so they hold big, easily recognized quantities: the puffy white mattress pads rolled up with their elasticized edges; the heavy, thick quilts of one season waiting to be pulled out in the early nights of winter, to be replaced by the light cotton summer blankets.

The sheets of the upper middle shelves testify to the passing of time, the changes in the family beds, an abundance of double-bed sheets, the oldest that dark olive green, that neon orange and pink of our first bed; then come the pastels, the sprigged and striped. On top are today's queen-sized white sheets, easily bleached of blood and other accidents of middle age.

The top shelf is a wonder of memory: water-bed sheets in a stiff synthetic fabric I hate to touch, in that outer-space swirl of the first teenage son; knitted pastel baby sheets to fit a cradle long since gone. There's even a blue flannel receiving blanket wrapped around William, my baby doll, left from childhood. He needs repairs; too fragile to sit out, he must be kept safe in that dark away from the air and light. Sometimes when I'm not thinking, I'll be rummaging up there on that awkward top shelf, and its contents shift so that suddenly I see his sweet rubber modeled face, his startled blue eyes staring down at me, his tiny mouth still in its eternal O of wanting, and I speak to him in a low voice and softly pat him.

Silent, Rainy

The pale whine of the refrigerator places
the kitchen against the far wall. The copper
rattle of the desk lamp is louder as I erase.
A door slams hollowly. The cat on my lap
while I write, the gray smell of drying fur,
the scrape of the pencil, cars slicking by.
Unevenly, the clock in the hall
knocks gears around the hour. In two
beats the dog stirs her metal
collar against the floor by my foot.
I will write
it is silent, rainy here.

Susan's Muses

Alarmina	The muse of waking early
Caffeina	The muse of making coffee
Persistina	The muse of sitting in the chair
Patienza	The muse of empty waiting
Silencia	The muse of quiet hope
Pushapena	The muse of putting pen to paper
Focusina	The blind and deaf muse of writing, no matter what

as long as I live:
straight lines, even spaces,
even-handed phrases
are not possible; the ragged
edge appeals to me,
the rough, unfinished open-ended line, the short &
long of it.
I've tried
sonnets,
twelve lines,
then a clever couplet,

& what was it I was trying to say?

Even haiku—

its seventeen syllables are
better, flexible but tight,
still *un* uneven.

I've tried
many schemes
to straighten it out,
fill the page,
one word after

another,

but then

I don't like to stop,

start, fill

in. Pardon

me, but I want words to

flow, bend, over-

lap, word waves splashing

up on each other, I want tides, storms,

oceans of words.

The Reception

The man on my left
asked what I do
The woman on my right
told us about her dog
The man on my left told us
about his mother's dog
The man on his left
left the circle
and another shorter man
joined us
The shorter man doesn't even like dogs
The noise rises around us
like spring runoff
pouring into the lagoon,
rising, pressing against the banks,
waiting for an opening

Beauty Shop

They hold their heads very still, waiting for the blunt cut. The talk in the mirror is of old boyfriends, of breaking up, of why they moved to the city. Their eyes never meet. The women in these elevated chairs come to be comforted. Their beauty waits for them in these mirrors, it moves across the room and back, like the sudden flash of light moving between signal mirrors held up to each other across miles of open water. Without any recognition, where does beauty begin? Here in this square bright room, every color appears on the glass shelves, the containers of mousse, gel, and spray in blue and turquoise and silver. The small, clever bottles of shining nail enamel: pink, orange, maroon, bright and gleaming red. In this room of women, the only man holds his head to one side and laughs loudest at his own jokes. A man can make a woman buy anything once he puts his clean, strong hands into her dark hair, feeling for body, feeling for the way it might fall naturally.

Lipstick

One finger at a time,
pulling gloves on, off,
closing a compact

like heels clicking
down the sidewalk,
winding the tube down, clicking
on the top

Remember Pink Clover,
Melon

There was one the exact clear
red purple
of a good hot borscht

But when the tip gets broken,
stuck inside the top
like soup blown from a pressure cooker—

Click of lipstick
and the sweet taste of it

The young girl in the laundromat waits for her family's clothes without using the phone through all the cycles. Outside, it is raining thickly into the streets and sidewalks; it covers the large glass window. The water takes on the color of its destination, gray for the asphalt gutter, sparkling and transparent traces for the glass. The washing machines hum and spin. The dryers along the wall form a massive bank of enormous portholes opening into a star-filled black enamel void. The closed ones look out into the tumbling whirlwind; each carries a detailed warning, hand-printed. Through the round glass, the multicolored clothes whirl counterclockwise for a time, then fall back the other way with a small sigh. The girl does not speak. She holds the heavy air in her mouth; she keeps sucking in the distinctions: soap flakes or detergent, warm or cold water, bleach, softener, liquid or powder.

The Cars of '57

Do you remember the '57 Chevies,
the Oldsmobile wings, the smooth
sound of fat tires, that leather seat

smell, chrome sweating summer nights
under Ford-convertible stars?
My favorite was the Starlight stick,

slick as a d.a., midnight-blue coupe,
ever ready and at the right time
to run out of gas.

The same cars pass me now;
the kids still drive them, the same
'57 metals, painted, lacquered, shined,

to the same different places and back:
Mel's, the Hot Shoppes, the Sugar Bowl.
Only human time on the glow-in-the-dark clocks

has stopped; only skin, knowledge,
kindness are stalled at this corner,
waiting for the light to change.

The Sailing Lesson

A mother brought her young daughter to take boating lessons on a narrow lake close to the sea. The mother had dreamed of sailing in a small open boat, its two triangular sails dipping in the wind. The daughter had a hard time getting up in time for the morning lessons. In the same narrow boat, the two of them laughed awkwardly, getting in each other's way, passing the tiller back and forth. Their boat became caught in the reeds, and they pulled themselves out of trouble hand over hand on the stiff, sharp stems. But in the next lesson they were placed in separate boats. The mother tried to keep her boat even with the other boat, but her boat kept zigzagging away; she was ignorant of any tacking maneuvers. She moved inevitably into the windless mud on the far side of the lake and watched the other boats bobbing across the water, their white sails filled with the offshore wind blowing over the darker ruffled surface. She watched them come about sharply and return to the boathouse; she watched them send the motor launch down the lake for the stragglers and mud sailors.

Brushing

Through a window, I watch a man brushing a young girl's hair, brushing so gently his strokes are a gift to his child, so young to hold her head so still, such stillness also a gift. Even this far away, I can see how gentle he is, no jerk at the end of the stroke, holding each strand as if connected.

When I used to wake in the morning, the snarls were like straw released out of nightmare: tangles, rats' tails, mare's nests. In the mirror, again and again I would try for the perfect part, brushing, combing, dividing, pulling the sections, braiding them back out of the way, tossing the braids over my shoulder, chewing the ends until they were stiff.

Once, when my hair was long and dark, a man could unpin the twisted, intricate knot, and I was undone, let loose like water falling, innocent strands flowing against his skin, arms, the rough tangles of his chest. There in the summer night, lying under its heavy liquid silence, breathing in its warmth, we were lost in that hair, in the even darkness of it.

I went to my wedding with one dark braid down my back, and it was soft against my skin and lay in the tender place between my shoulder blades nothing touches in quite the same way.

No one touched my father's head, his thinning hair that looked so soft, his fine, beautiful, clean, smooth head. He never touched ours, he never could have brushed, brushed, brushed down the back one hundred strokes. The man in the window is still brushing his daughter's hair, his dark head bent over hers in the light.

Partial Military Honors

I can never get used to the blunt echo
of the shots.
The three black rifles against the sky
break the shuddering afternoon in half.
My father was dying all my life,
in the Pacific, the Aleutians, Korea,
on the highway, over and over; each leaving
was a dying. Coming back was a dying, too.

Left behind, waving into the bitter wind
at the slowly turning side of his ship, waving
as the gray boats tugged at it, waving
at the curtained window as the car pulled away.
I never wanted to be left.
What sound is more final than an empty street?

The young guards stumble in the wind
and count the folds of the flag. His old classmates
wait bareheaded for the same clear notes again.
They stand at attention so often
now, over and over again, listening for the shots.
Their eyes water in the wind.

In my own mourning, I can eat, open the mail, wash dishes—

but not talk, make phone calls, make lists.
The memory is blank.
I feel the too-wet soil of winter
and wait to plant.

On this coast, the ocean breaks in slow winter swells.
The boys hammer in the basement,
the sound like muffled shots.
Soup bubbles quietly, and the corn bread rises
to crumble in our hands.

In Wet Weather

In wet weather walking in the wet in the wetter weather wild wind in the wild wet wind and rain raining rain my round rain round raining rainwater walking rain raining weather my wet weather work boots my wet boots my ankle leather boots walking in my wet boots to your wet stoop to your dry to your drying step out of the weather through the wind and wet to your step my boots my wet brown boots worn boots my soft my worn wet brown boots worn boots my soft wet leather boots my wet string laces knotted fraying my ends knotted wet wound in wet weather 'round my wrapped-up ankle and tied twice untying the laces the twisted tangles outside the wet inside leave the wet my wet weather my wet into warm inside leave my boots my tangle my rain my weather walking wet weather raining wet weather into warm your warm

Winter Storm

I woke in the dark, the clock's *blink-blink*: the power's out.
No news forecast, it's here, this storm that shoves us,
thuds and blows and groans, and doors slam shut.
Still, I start out across the city inside my car's thin walls,

and the wind moves us, rocks us in uneven gusts,
and the rain slashes, whips, the rain sheets us blind,
and traffic slows to slosh the puddled, flooded streets.
We ford deep intersections, creep and slog

past whole trees down, huge balls of branches, sideways
splintered wood, and chain saws shriek,
and tree men, happy in their danger, laugh
and shout into the wind. My wipers swish and scrape,
the wind gusts rip, and roar, and shake, and

one umbrella lifts its bright inverted blossom.

Moon Aquarium

Creed

I believe in the moon aquarium
and in her stars
swimming in the liquid sky

and in the lobster of the night
clacking her one black claw
the one that always comes too close
in this personal space

I believe in stumble freefall
in boot-ring asteroids and
comets that scrape and crack

I believe in the sofa madrone
the babushka of suck
the tabulation of the reeboks
and the pluck everlasting

Bull's Head

After a Persian sculpture in the Museum of Fine Arts, Boston

For a thousand years this has saved you
from certain loss, dismemberment.

Not your bent horns, gold wound 'round,
the gold spheres of your eyes
ringed and ringed again with gold.

Not the gold circles, whorls of muzzle hair,
clustered beads of gold
in the short hairs on your broad nose.

Not even your great golden ears,
smoothed, flattened, curved scoops
to pour my words
into your hollow darkness,
darkness of the darkness.

In each of a thousand lives,
it has saved you
(no molten gold, no forgotten dark power).

It is sweetness
we hold and remember—

your gentle, gentle face

Invocation

O Pig Mother,
Dainty red eyes, wedgie trotters,
Our rowdy sow—

O crossbred queen,
Mother of thousands,
Lift your slit ear, your cartilaginous snout!

Ruler of the Swine Barn,
O Mother Pignut, Earthnut, *Carya glabra*,
May your children ever circle and dart,

May their numbers fill the lists,
Their names roll from the tongues of judges,
May their every piggy expression charm you.

O Pig Mother,
Crossbred queen,
Our rowdy sow!

Estate Sale

It has the smooth finish of fine-grind
sandpaper, rooms unused, like narrow-gauge track.
There are no loose boards, no slack
wires. This house was his rind,
kept tight. He had a mind of certain order,
of files far back, of categories in place, of lists.
We lack everything and cannot see we're blind.

In death he lifts the dust Martini,
the goal, the end he was striving toward,
slightly chilled by the marble graves.

In this house we feel the pulse of the sea
playing empty rooms like some harpsichord,
the checkered floor rolling in gentle waves.

Final Odors

In the stalls, the fragile pasta is piled into a paper bag. It is the color of the moon. Pale sardine cans shine in an old lady's hand. Gesticulating at a door, a man scrapes open a slight, apoplectic fish with a nasty wound; the arteries sometimes appear weak and nervous. In the dark hallway, a boy appears, country cousin to the fish. Outdoors alone, he puts away the key that is always too small for his room. Leaving the slight odor of ammonia pouring into the long, humid streets, he is held by the glimmer of cabbages, of beans and carrots grown in the sludge. His hand is open; reaching, he takes a bite. Sometimes he has a vision of her short, treacherous skirt, the color of the fish shining hard for him there at the door.

Skogsparti: On Behalf of the Skogs

A mistranslation of a poem by Tomas Tranströmer

Papa always said he came from just small tradespeople, salad merchants, that was all. That he was also such a man. That they made it big just by selling hog-fat pork bellies, so sums would bulge out of their wallets, such huge sums that it must be due to the stars or the springtime, when feckless men were otherwise afraid. For his family, marriage arrangements only increased the good luck every springtime. And the spells cast by envious radar were felt only as a general tingling: the housewives could make forecasts from them, about which deals would fall to them down out of heaven. This was the kind of man for whom vanda orchids were a sign. This was that sweet sort lying open like plowed earth. This was the wanderer, the one who would travel for weeks, for years, searching for exalted halls, strange nectars.

My fat papa, sweet puppet, can he fly up there, hang by some strange skill learned from our hidden forefathers, Papa neither so melancholy nor so crazy? In the dark barnlight a whispering crouches, tempting us. In mildness, we are all Skogs.

To the Six Appearances

The door of the mirror is opened
and the appearances begin mumbling, "After you," "After you,"
unaware, precisely, of how many of them there are.

The first of them at last sits down and, looking up
at the rest, notices for the first time since spring
how tired his face has grown on the shoulders of
the others who continue to parade past him,
unaware of his Scottish ancestry and rich, noble brogue.
How tired his face had grown
constantly smiling and smiling,
each remaining tooth shining
in the sun. All he could do was
eat round, firm-fleshed grapes, piercing the skins
with his few remaining
teeth, drinking down the sun.
This was one of the few pleasures left to him.
It brought back his rich dreams of the tropics,
a time in his life when
his superb tan and extensive collection of teeth
had made him a figure of respect and envy
among the townsfolk.

But now age slowed him,
and Death the Hunter rose high
every night in the sky above his house.

Berkeley No. 20 by Richard Diebenkorn

Mud gray drying on the flats,
a map of the old days
lying under the real
(what did you expect?)

there
the dark horizon line not quite straight,
curve of the earth,
gray water, sky, pale fog, clouds,
bridges, something of bridges and last light

old brown weeds by the road,
then silver iridescence,
oil slick and pale orange
headlights in the dusk

the distant splash of puddles,
other cars down the hill
coming closer, the hill its own line,
lead black refracted,
then here at our feet
indented square black curb,
sidewalk roadway

this gray day when brown is warm,
when peach is bright
                    hot   fast

Le Repos sous le lilas

It is warm, summer at last.
We've found our white dresses,
washed them, hung them
wet and slick with starch,
then pressed every flounce and ruffle.
We've new straw hats with broad brims
curved just so, black ribbons smoothed around.
Late afternoon
under the lilacs, heavy with fragrance
and sweet shade. It is cool,
a cave of pink and dusty green.
Your chubby legs nearly reach the edge of my skirt;
the branches almost touch your hat,
yet in this dim confusion,
the dove-gray colors of the shadows,
we know above us there is light,
the sun just catching new green tips,
the palest blossoms not quite open.
The day is not yet over just above our heads;
not yet the dew rising in the grass,
not yet the night wind from the river,
a bird still talking to herself
deep in the darkening blossoms.
We will go in,
but not yet.

Water Is My Only Home

Sonnet

Old dog spread out to the lazy sun,
faint tinny sound of a marching band
from the open window of the house behind.
Limp purple leaves shimmer in the emptying
branches of the old plum. Fallen drought fruits
on the dead grass are hollow homes to the jointed
gray crustaceous roly polies, sweet caves for yellow jackets.
Sitting here on these steps, I know that smell.
Every fall it came from the old orchard on our steep Virginia hill.
Even from those dying trees we could never pick them all.
Jays and sparrows came to peck the skin, loose
and sweet. They carried off every hope of wholeness,
the perfect finished thing. The pain of the possible.
This haze and buzz, remembering that ripe, dead smell.

Water Is My Only Home

Born beside the Pacific in wartime San Diego,
my first swim was with the White Swan soap,
the shiny tub, the swirly silver drain.
Later I waited for my sisters
at the North Beach Crystal Plunge
before our long trip across the country,
away from the ocean, away from home.

We drove for days, across bridges and rivers,
up the hill to that old Southern house.
The only water was the creek at the bottom of the hill.
Those were the years they closed the swimming pools,
afraid of polio, afraid of integration.

When I was seven, we moved across the ocean.
For weeks out of sight of land
on the USS *Andrew Jackson*, too small for troops,
we kids had the run of the ship.
At night the dark was warm as the ship moved
through water; we could feel it,
breathe it, all that water.
I was moving through my home.

On an island, still a fish, I learned to swim,
to dive in the chlorine pool in Makalapa,
my sisters on the sides, flirting—

underwater days, mermaid games.
We drove around the island
up the Pali road, and stopped the car to watch
the waterfalls fall up,
then wound down to that long golden beach
I'd never leave, the clear, warm ocean
rocking me all day,
my only home.

Then back to the mainland,
the dry hours, days, years of school and work,
but still I found water, pools of summer,
my turn to flirt beside the pool.

I swam through high school, college,
on the women's swim team, raced and won.
My hair froze on those bitter nights
as I ran back to the dorm.
I fell in love beside the stormy ocean,
rushing waves and clear starred skies.

My life changed by the ocean.
I made my first child there;
we made our home by water.
He's a swimmer too, and still,
water is my only home.

Great Blue

Early evening, blue shifting to gray along
the edge of the lagoon in the shadows

still water, still air

a heron waiting
and
          another
                    still there
          below

We climbed Bolinas Ridge early, walking together, silent in the dust and warm smell of bay laurel, in the shadows of the tall pines and golden-tipped, thick-branched cypresses. We climbed higher still to look down on those trees, and all morning we heard the rustling confusion and saw the rough gray, haphazard nests below us. Everywhere, bird-family history was going on, the late lovers courting their chosen one with the clacking of big sticks, the tired parents coming and going, beaks outstretched, dripping some delicate morsel. And the ugly naked newborns, squirming, squawking, four or five to a nest, thrusting their sharp beaks up again and again.

Beaks open, they grab, gulp, clack,
stretch and scrabble,
jab and poke;

push against the hard sticks, held
in the thick branches,
they hop, hobble,
knob legs catch and scratch,
wing feathers bent,

until one day they struggle, fall,
          wings stretch out and
flapping slow and heavy
          soar
past the branches, trees,
above the grasses, then
the cold splash, spraying,
feet down into the slick
warm mud,
          and wait
for a quick silver shape,
then the first plunge and miss,
and wait and wait and
stab
          that first time
          caught, that

ah, sweet wet salty flesh

Three Planets

At midsummer this city holds our weather
like a gray shawl around us.
One day much like another,
the nights cool and damp,
the mornings white and thick with cold.
The afternoon wind kicks the papers up
against the curb, lays them against garage doors.

Now the city waits
while the planets move around each other.
Jupiter, weighted gold, quick Mars,
and Venus with her liquid light—
three planets
loom above the neighbor's silent house,
over the end of the street, above the quiet bay.

Day, night, another tide, another
moon phase, and our slow and certain course swings
back around the far side of the sun.
It begins here among the long, dry days;
the shadows stretch into the afternoon,
the dry hills, the dying grass.
The weeds have gone black, the foxtails bristle;
their sharp seeds catch on everything.

The little black cat blinks and closes
his second eyelid
          swollen against the barb.

And we know that what will follow is less
and less of the same; we know
beyond these circling planets,
loss is waiting.

This Once the Eclipse

This once the eclipse:
ominous, like a coming storm,

the sky turned strange
all at once, everywhere.

I've watched so many sunsets
here at the western edge;

this time a strange wrongness,
a solemn darkness hovering.

No wonder people once believed
in the music of the spheres:

perfect alignment,
circles over circles.

Now the tiniest moon is passing.
Look in its shadow,

away from the light, so much light,
such dangerous light,

only visible at this time, in this place,
with luck.

The Stairs

The stairs are a room unlike any other. Not even hallways have that complex light, that bending and folded space. Stairs hold secrets beyond the turn. The steps creak and groan with every passing: the heavy, slow, unseeing step of long use; the quick sound of a child in a hurry, falling against the riser and bruising herself. In the silence late at night, a long-legged youth passes his parents' closed door and presses his hot skin against the wall of the stairs, taking every other step, stretching to miss the loud ones. It takes him a long time in the dark to get out without making a sound on the wooden stairs.

If the stairs are spiral, the steps fan out in petals like a zinnia, like a dahlia, first narrow at the center, then wide. It is a simple curve, the inner line of a chambered nautilus—not circles within circles, but ovals connected at the edge. The curving banister ascends, pulled by its dark wood up toward the top, out of sight. On the stairs, looking down from the top, only the first landing at the curve is visible. At the bottom, the unseeable waits.

Night

Then,
the only one awake,
I lay in the silence,
knowing our parents had gone out,
knowing my sisters were asleep,
        listening
to the house move, hearing
sounds I never heard in daytime.
It wasn't the cat coming down the hall,
or any other living thing,
just that strangely unknowable
        sound.

Now
I sleep hard when I can,
or wake to the familiar noises
of the city around me
        and sleep again.

Sometimes, though,
I lie awake
with the fear of what's coming,
that long silence from within,
forever the little bones and tubes freezing up,
and no sound can tell me
        where I am, or what's coming next.

The Radiation Waiting Room

They bring us to this pastel room,
point to the lockers,
point to the dressing rooms.
It could almost be a gym,
only there's a wheelchair, there's *Health News*,
there's a complicated flower jigsaw puzzle,
there are romance novels to borrow
in case you will be returning often.
We change into gowns that tie in the back;
some of us get to keep on our shirts,
some our pants;
we all wear shoes.
Those of us who have come so often
wait comfortably,
take care of the new ones,
offer answers, directions, suggestions.
Only we are careful not to say
how long we've been coming
or what we have or
what they've done
or are about to do.

Too Much Sleep

Why do I not have many dreams now?
Is it too much sleeping?

Or if I do dream,
            what is it I dream of?
Do my dead appear,
            is it my father?
But if I did, if it were,
            I think I'd remember,
though I can't remember much of anything
            since the surgery.

Is it my mother, then?
        Those times I feel
                an easeful sleep,
              is it dreaming then,
            a sound, perhaps
              just her voice
                I almost hear?
Or can I only remember
        the dreams from before the diagnosis,
        the ones I wrote down
            in the maze-moment of waking? So now each
              any
                memory, name, place,
                  even finding the keys . . .

Do I dream of just the tangible,
  a taste, bittersweet,
  a faint, familiar scent?

The Next Day

Counting back to get to
the day after the day of the world not ending,

back from Tuesday, the Christmas Day feast,
and Monday, and Sunday, the frantic shopping,
back to that Saturday—it rained, I think.

And forgetting it was the day after,
I was glad to mostly stay inside,
just resting and sleeping and napping
in those weeks of chemo,
going out each day
only to get the shots of Neupogen,

doing all I could to live,
forgetting it was the day after the day of
not ending—

all that I did, the trip to the clinic,
the pinch, the rush of the shot,
the drive back through the rain,
the quiet resting,
all, all adds to this day,
one more day

after the day of not ending.

Each Moss Sleeps

The curtain closes, the play is ended—
walking home in the dark, who will have the last words?

The barnacles cling to the bottom of the boat;
each moss sleeps inside the darkness.

The violets nestle in the shade and damp;
wings stretch, veins pulse with the beat and glow.

The lamp hangs down before the woman sitting alone in the dark.
The moon stays open into the night.

To Sing and Sing Again

In the last poems
in the last things I can write
there is a word map to remember
crossing lines and nodules
connecting all the places and people and moments
everything that mattered

Probably it's hard for someone else to read
my life's
not exactly linear
and when you hold this paper
my words will move around
down

trying to catch each, every thing
the good bread the sweetness
the tang of morning fog
the sounds shimmering in the dark
softer now
as I try to catch them
one after another like the last
fireflies the last
silence

The Right Angle for Heaven

I wish I could believe
angels are everywhere
around us and come to us
when we need—
Grandmother, Mary, Helen, and Alice,
their arms filled with baskets
of tiny red strawberries and ripe peaches,
their summer hats at the right
          angle for heaven.

Maybe they will bring me
my own hat, a yellow straw one
with a dark ribbon, a bunch of scarlet cherries,
and then I too will follow,
pausing near the sign in the waiting room
near the curved golden benches
of the Southern Station, listening
for the conductor to call out,
"Richmond, Atlanta, Memphis, Athens, Paradise."
Then rising, without thinking,
I will choose my destination.

About the Author

Susan Herron Sibbet was born in San Diego in 1942. She and her four sisters grew up on both coasts of the United States and in Hawaii during their father's various postings as an admiral in the United States Navy. Susan attended Brown University and the University of Virginia as an undergraduate, then Northwestern University as a Woodrow Wilson Fellow, where she earned a master's degree and completed the course work for a PhD. She and her husband, David, raised their family in San Francisco, where she was awarded an MFA from San Francisco State University. Susan was also a Bunting Fellow at Radcliffe/Harvard, and held writing residencies at Soapstone in Oregon and at the Headlands Center for the Arts in California.

Susan was the author of two poetry chapbooks—*The Weight Is Comforting* and *Under Suspicion of Sisters*—and a coauthor of a third, *Suspensions*; she was also the author of a combined poetry collection and cookbook, *Burnt Toast and Other Recipes*. A founding member of Sixteen Rivers Press, she published her first full-length collection of poetry, *No Easy Light*, with the press in 2004. Her novel, *The Constant Listener*, a fictional memoir by Theodora Bosanquet, the amanuensis to Henry James, was published in 2016 by Ohio University Press. She was devoted to California Poets in the Schools, where she served both as acting director and president of the board and taught for many years in the CPITS program for younger children.

Susan died in 2013 after a long struggle with cancer; her ashes were scattered in the Pacific Ocean at Kirby Cove, just outside the Golden Gate.

Sixteen Rivers Press is a shared-work, nonprofit poetry collective dedicated to providing an alternative publishing avenue for San Francisco Bay Area poets. Founded in 1999 by seven writers, the press is named for the sixteen rivers that flow into San Francisco Bay.

SAN JOAQUIN• FRESNO • CHOWCHILLA • MERCED • TUOLUMNE
STANISLAUS • CALAVERAS • BEAR • MOKELUMNE • COSUMNES • AMERICAN
YUBA • FEATHER • SACRAMENTO • NAPA • PETALUMA

Design: Carolyn Miller

Display type: Gill Sans Light

Text type: Adobe Garamond Pro

Printed on reycled paper by McNaughton & Gunn